This book belongs to

Wynn Norwood

969-4969

THE WONDERFUL WORLD OF HORSES

THE
WONDERFUL
WORLD OF
HORSES

Matthew Long

octopus

CONTENTS

First published 1976 by
Octopus Books Limited
59 Grosvenor Street, London W1

ISBN 0 7064 0564 1

© 1976 Octopus Books Limited

Produced by Mandarin Publishers Limited
22a Westlands Road, Quarry Bay, Hong Kong

Printed in Hong Kong

MAN AND HORSE

Fifty million years ago there existed a small animal known to palaeontologists as Eohippus. Over the ages this fox-sized creature evolved into Equus, the horse as we now know it. Cave paintings show the horse as a hunted creature but gradually man realized that it could be more than just a source of food. He learned to harness it for work and, much later, to ride upon its back, enabling him to travel over greater distances.

The mutual trust and respect on which the comradeship of horse and man is founded has survived countless wars and disasters and the inevitable indignities of a servant-master relationship. The horse has remained steadfast and loyal over thousands of years but has never lost his personality or the individual characteristics that make him such a fascinating and noble beast.

Today the horse is considered mainly as a source of pleasure but it is only recently that the horse as a worker has disappeared from our everyday life and in many parts of the world he still does a job where no machine can ever replace him. It is hard to believe that horses were used in war as recently as the Second World War. It is easier to remember them much further back in history. Before the invention of the internal combustion engine and steam vehicles they were the unrivalled means of transport through much of the world and played an extremely important part in men's lives.

Interest in breeding was developed very early for a horse was often a man's most valued possession. Statues and paintings, legends and myths have honoured the horse, for no other creature has been so useful or given itself so entirely to the service of humanity.

The horse's nature is to serve but never to become the slave of man. With a toss of his head or a sudden quick movement he can make a fool of us if he wishes. If he no longer wants someone on his back he lets him know in no uncertain manner, and in a second the rider is on the ground.

Contact with horses can teach us patience, tolerance and perseverance. Calmness and quietness are also essential, for the horse is a highly sensitive creature and basically frightened of sudden assaults on his tranquillity. Police horses and the ceremonial mounts of cavalry soldiers undergo a long and arduous training to acquaint them with all types of disturbance and noise.

Many horses become strongly attached to their owners and have a distinctive character and a good sense of fun. If after a strenuous two or three days at a show a horse is turned out in his familiar paddock he will show his pleasure by squealing, bucking and rolling for a few minutes before settling down to graze peacefully. Horses are gregarious and pine if they do not have a companion, even though they may graze at opposite ends of their field. All sorts of habits and vices can develop when a horse gets bored with its own company, and many will develop odd little tricks to amuse themselves, and you too if you watch them for long enough. Some learn to untie ropes with amazing ease and a clip and chain can be the only answer if you are to be sure of keeping your horse in one place for more than five minutes. Horses have been known to remove their stable companions' head collars, and, if given the chance, systematically to remove every article of grooming kit from a box and deposit them on the stable floor. Many horses learn how to undo the bolts of the stable door and gain their freedom. At first this is usually just by chance, after the horse has been playing with the bolt, enjoying the rattling noise. It does not take the horse long to realize how it opened the door. A safety clip on the bolt puts an end to that.

Horses are vegetarians but there are exceptions. A taste in buttons has been known—one particular horse could not resist coat buttons within his reach, and many horses enjoy stealing clothing or anything else that takes their fancy and prance off with their prize, delighting to tease the owner by dashing off every time he comes near and attempts to retrieve it.

When the mood takes a horse, even the smallest scrap of paper fluttering in the hedge is an excuse for a display of fun and games. Many horses will play the fool to test the rider's reactions. On passing a certain spot on a familiar ride, your horse may shy sideways as if a herd of elephants was about to emerge from behind the nearest tree. But this is the same tree that you have been passing for months and surely there is nothing different? To your horse, who by this time resembles the fiery steed of mediaeval paintings with his distended nostrils, arched neck and high tail carriage, something is decidedly different. There is no logical explanation except that this is a sensitive animal with a mind of his own and it is possible that he sees things which we cannot see or understand.

Horses were introduced to Australia by European settlers but the Australian aborigine, like the North American Indian, has proved a fine horseman with a deep understanding of the animal. Indeed, the Australian stockman (*right*) has much in common with the North American cowboy.

6

Horsemanship, largely developed by the nomadic peoples of Central Asia, was taken by them to China where horses were highly prized. Chinese art presents many fine studies of the horse in sculpture, bronze, painting and exquisite porcelain like this valuable piece.

The ancient Greeks began to learn the skills of horsemanship about 800 BC but they had no knowledge of the saddle or the stirrup, although simple reins were used and they later began to use a saddlecloth. Horses figure in Greek mythology and were highly valued. Horse racing became a popular sport at Olympiads and other gatherings. This fine vase with its study of spirited stallions and their riders (*right*) may have been a prize to the winner of a race.

Although it dates from the time of imperial Rome, and shows accoutrements from that period, this fine bronze (*below*) probably represents Alexander the Great, one of the great figures in Greek history. Alexander the Great was the son of the King of Macedonia in Northern Greece, and from an early age he showed a great sympathy in his handling of horses and perhaps one of the most famous stories to be associated with this great warrior involves his charger, Bucephalus. Alexander acquired this magnificent black steed when he was a mere boy of thirteen; the horse was declared unrideable but the young Alexander was able to win the horse's confidence and used him for many years on his arduous and lengthy campaigns.

An old print of a Buffalo Hunt. The Indians are riding Mustangs, the small wild horses which were descended from horses taken to America by the first Spanish settlers.

The great cities of the world have many fine equestrian statues commemorating historic figures. This statue in Paris (*left*) shows Joan of Arc who was reputed to be a brilliant horsewoman able to handle animals only considered suitable for men.

Colonel Byerley's charger (*below*), the 'Byerley Turk', founded a dynasty of English racehorses at the end of the seventeenth century: he was the great-grandfather of the famous racehorse Eclipse, unbeaten in his racing career.

Some horses have a tremendous sense of humour. This one (*right*) likes to swing a broom between his teeth so that he appears to be sweeping his own yard.

Wild stallions will fight each other for lordship over a herd of mares and domesticated colts still go through the mock battles (*below*) which would have prepared them for adulthood.

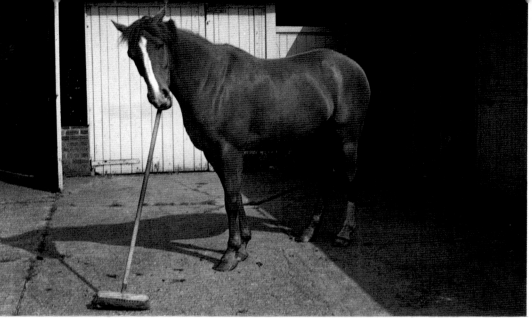

Naturally enough, horses have most fun
playing with each other, and at the same
time they will be doing themselves a lot
of good. These Thoroughbred yearlings
(*above*) are gaining strength and stamina
for their arduous careers as racehorses,
and developing their gawky frames into
the sleek muscular bodies capable of
racing at high speeds on the track. They
are from the Ocala Stud in Florida, a
centre of Thoroughbred breeding which
has come to the fore over the last twenty
years in America.

Horses love having a good roll (*left*),
particularly when they are hot after a
hard day's work. Rolling seems to be
infectious among horses—once one is
down in the field, others follow suit. The
old horse dealers used to say that a horse
was worth another twenty guineas if he
could roll right over from one side to the
other.

The Australian sun has scorched out
most of the goodness from the grass, but
these mares and foals have been well fed
and cared for on a Victoria Stud (*right*).
Victoria is one of the richest Australian
states, and when its population quickly
multiplied with the discovery of gold, the
site of Melbourne was chosen as a good
place for a village. Now it is the capital of
course, and is the scene of the Melbourne
Cup, the country's most important
classic. Despite the inevitably firm
ground, some steeplechases are included
in programmes there. Melbourne Cup
day is like a state holiday, when the
racing fever takes hold of people who take
no interest in other races, and
thousands of enthusiasts flock to the
racecourse from all over the country.

BREEDS OF THE WORLD

The many different breeds and types of horses recognized in the world today include giants weighing more than a ton, tiny animals less than a yard high, spotted horses, golden horses, those named after their outstanding walking gait, and streamlined racing machines capable of galloping the 35 mph requisite for the Derby Stakes.

Most of the older continental breeds trace back in some degree to the Andalusian of the Middle Ages, since Spanish horses were considered to be of the highest quality and prized throughout Europe. They originated from the crosses between local Spanish mares and the Barb stallions brought in by Moorish invaders of the eighth century, and were powerful, high-actioned horses with a very abundant mane and tail which they still retain to some extent, though they are now lighter and speedier animals than their ancestors of the Middle Ages. The modern Andalusian is almost as well known as the Spanish Arab, and the mares were used for breeding all over Europe.

Another breed which penetrated over Europe in the sixteenth and seventeenth centuries and to which many modern horses are related is the Lipizzaner. These horses originally came from Yugoslavia where they are still used extensively for farm work and are prized for their stamina and co-operation. They are also bred in Austria and Hungary and have been well known for centuries for their magnificent ceremonial and parade-ground work.

After the last war stocks of all the various continental breeds were sadly depleted, and to strengthen them and to build up their numbers to meet the growing demand for general purpose horses, judicious cross breeding with Lipizzaners and in particular Britain's Cleveland Bay took place in many countries. The Cleveland Bay is often claimed to be the only pure-bred general purpose horse without a trace of Heavy horse blood, and originated in Yorkshire as a pack horse known as 'Chapman's Horse' which carried trinkets and merchandise over the dales. Sturdy and short-legged, the mares were first crossed with Thoroughbred sires in the eighteenth century, and by the early part of the nineteenth century the Cleveland Bay was a tall, showy carriage horse very much in demand to draw the dashing vehicles of the wealthy around London and all over the country. They make first-class heavyweight hunters, and crossed with quality mares the stallions sire excellent jumpers which are often seen in the show ring. They were first imported into America in the early part of the nineteenth century.

One of the breeds that was strengthened with Cleveland Bays is the Oldenburg, a German horse rather heavier than the Cleveland but the most popular German horses are the Trakehners. They have been famous for their endurance and courage ever since the horses of the well-known Trakehner Stud in East Prussia undertook a 900-mile trek to escape from the advancing Russian armies. They are more elegant than the Hanoverians and make excellent riding and showing horses.

The Swedish Saddle Horse is one of the most recently developed of the all purpose riding horses, and contains Arabian, Thoroughbred, Trakehner and Lipizzaner blood. They have been selectively bred since the beginning of the nineteenth century for temperament as well as conformation, and are as a result a very elegant, equable riding horse, up to weight and with the scope for international competing, and equally popular with civilians, the Army and the police.

The settlers in the eastern colonies of America imported most of their horses from England, and under the different conditions and by selective and cross breeding of these, combined at times with some Mustang blood, they gradually evolved the many distinctive American breeds of today.

The American Standardbred, of Thoroughbred type but sturdier, with a longer back and shorter legs and averaging 15.2 hands, is the outstanding harness racer in the world today. It is very fast and has great endurance, and can be either a trotter, which has a diagonal action, or a pacer, which moves its legs laterally like a camel. Although these horses possess a lot of Thoroughbred blood, they also trace back to Harddravers, the Dutch trotting breed, and to a famous Norfolk Trotter imported in 1822.

Hackney Horses are also harness trotters, of an old British breed with much the same origins as racing trotters, but their brilliant, extravagant action is nowadays confined almost exclusively to the show ring.

The American Saddle Horse, sometimes called the Kentucky Saddler, makes an excellent riding horse for most purposes, but is now bred chiefly for the show ring where it is often an admirable exponent of the five gaits, trot, canter, rack, slow gait and walk. These horses have great beauty and tremendous presence, and as well as being the showiest of almost all breeds they also have gentle natures and considerable stamina.

A versatile American breed that is equally popular in Canada and rapidly becoming so in Australia is the Quarter Horse, an old type used for Quarter Mile racing in the eighteenth century, but only registered in 1940. When ousted from racing by more conventional tracks and the Thoroughbred racer, the Quarter Horse pattern was preserved in a slightly modified form in the southwest, principally in Texas where they are now exten-

The Arab (*above*) is the oldest and purest breed developed by man. Drawings and carvings go back many thousand years and there are even records of named horses 3000 years BC. Breeders have guarded their ancient qualities with fanaticism, maintaining their fine features, dish face, neat ears, wide dark eyes and flared nostrils.

The last remaining link with the prehistoric horse is thought to be *Equus Przevalski* (*right*). Przevalsky's horse still roams wild on the plains of Mongolia and many more can be seen in zoos all over the world. The colour of these horses is predominantly dun, red dun and brown dun with the characteristic mealy nose and eyes. Another strange feature is the upright growth of their spiky manes.

The spirited Lusitano (*above*) is a breed indigenous to Portugal. Once used as cavalry mounts they still do light agricultural work and are trained for the bullring.

The Selle Français (*left*) is the result of crosses between indigenous French mares and Arabs, Thoroughbreds and trotters. This stallion, like most in France, is owned by the government.

sively bred. They are low and compact with great muscular strength, particularly in the thighs and quarters, and possess an intelligent, calm temperament. They make first-class all-round saddle horses and the finer strains are still raced over short distances, usually the traditional quarter of a mile, a sport that has spread from the States to Canada, and is starting up in Australia.

For working stock the Quarter Horse has few equals with his speed, stamina, ability to make lightning turns and instinctive cattle sense.

Within the last fifty years a vogue has started for promoting and registering horses and ponies of the same specific colouring, although often of different type.

Appaloosas are the most well known of the American spotted breeds, and this particular colouring was developed by the Nez Percé Indians, a tribe living around the Palouse River districts of the far north-west. The horses have a particoloured skin, and striped hooves. The patterns of spots vary, the most usual being dark spots scattered over a white patch on hips and loins.

The metallic glint of a Palomino horse is perhaps the most attractive colouring of all. In the fifteenth century these golden horses are said to have been much prized by the Spanish Queen Ysabella, and they are sometimes known as Ysabellas.

There are few breeds of horse or pony that have not at some time been improved with Arabian blood. The history of these lovely animals with their distinctive concave profiles, tapering muzzles, broad foreheads and big, luminous dark eyes dates back to the seventh century. They remained unsullied because they come of a relatively small stock of much prized horses, fanatically inbred, culled, and kept 'asil' (pure-bred) for centuries by the desert tribes. When the Arabs set out on conquest they augmented their cavalry with local horses and their stallions bred with these, helping to found the general type of 'hot-blood' horse established from North Africa to Spain, and in India and the Near East. However alien horses were never taken back to adulterate their own pure Arab strains.

Very few of the cherished Arabian mares ever left their country of origin, but through the centuries many stallions were exported. Foreign breeders therefore often built up studs using domestic mares and there are not many of the true, ancient blood-lines left. Some famous studs, however, in Britain, the U.S.A. and else-

where outside Arabia, were built on pure-bred Arabian horses, though they possibly are not considered 'asil' in Arab estimation, since different feeding and environment often produce much larger animals than the original and in some countries, particularly America, the big Arabian horse in any case is considered preferable. Although these retain many of the qualities of their breed, they differ materially from the smaller pure desert-bred horses of the Royal Jordanian Stud, which are now world famous.

The Thoroughbred is a comparatively young breed originated in England by the crossing of a few imported Arabian stallions with good Hunter mares, and there are now famous studs in many countries including New Zealand, Australia, the U.S.A. and France, where the admirable cross of Thoroughbred/Arabian called Anglo-Arab, now breeds true. In conformation, grace of line and speed the Thoroughbred has no equal, the name is now synonymous with racehorse, and these horses are used extensively to develop or improve other breeds. But Thoroughbreds do tend to be nervous and highly strung, and though their quality and jumping ability fit them in many ways for sports other than racing, a Thoroughbred cross, often a half- or three-quarter-bred, usually proves more suitable for eventing and show jumping.

In Australia many modern breeders are concentrating on Thoroughbred and light bloodstock in preference to the versatile type of animals called Walers from New South Wales. The foundation stock of these horses in-

The Quarter Horse (*above*) of America developed from a seventeenth-century cross between Spanish and English horses. It was a popular horse for short races of about 440 yards, known as 'quarter milers', and the name has stuck. The English settlers missed going to race meetings and started their own informal sprint races between two horses on their land and even up the main streets of towns. They bred horses suitable which were compactly built and had well-built shoulders and quarters to give them the power for a quick start and speed. The breed is very versatile and has remained popular for short races and all types of rodeo contests such as cutting, roping, barrel racing and bull-dogging.

The Furioso (*right*) is an Hungarian breed created from an English foundation stallion from which it takes its name. Striking, all-purpose horses they make good-looking, active, saddle horses and shine in trotting competitions and races.

cluded hot-blooded Cape Horses brought in by traders in the late eighteenth century, and later they gained strength and stamina from cross breeding with heavier animals, often imported Clydesdales. They make good stock and riding horses, do well on endurance rides and are first-class jumpers—in 1940 a Waler made the then world high jump of 8 ft 4 ins. They also have the not always enviable reputation of being better at bucking than American Broncos. But although there are still Walers at work on many sheep and cattle stations in their native land, and some units of the Australian Mounted Police still ride them, this utilitarian type is now unfashionable, which is a pity in view of their long and distinguished history.

A beautiful Palomino (*left*), given the freedom of his paddock, canters in perfect style with neck arched and head well tucked in. The Palomino is not a breed but a colour: golden with flaxen mane and tail. Its origin may be Arab and date back to prehistory.

The Appaloosa (*below left*) is an unusually marked horse which may come in several coat patterns. The name is derived from the Palouse area in Idaho, home of the Nez Percé Indians. Some specimens are brilliantly and strikingly spotted black on grey all over. They also made some of the best working ponies possessing particularly good 'cow sense'. Although the tribe was wiped out in battle the horses survived and have become one of the most popular breeds in America. This one is being trained in the corral of a big ranch to be obedient and accurate at speed.

A beautiful Arab mare and her fine foal (*right*) carry a proud ancestry. For many people, the Arab epitomizes the horse in all its glory. The proud bearing and presence of the Arab is unmistakable. Renowned for its stamina, beauty, soundness and speed, it remains one of the purest of the equine breeds.

The English Thoroughbred (*right*) is almost synonymous with the word racehorse. The distinguished breed sprang from three great Arab horses at the beginning of modern horse racing in the early eighteenth century: the Darley Arabian, the Godolphin Barb and the Byerley Turk.

The wild Mustangs of North America (*below*) are not indigenous horses but are descended from horses which went feral, originally taken to the continent by European settlers. Running wild, with neither selective breeding or grain feeding they degenerated in size but still retain the toughness, reliance and resistance to disease of their forebears. The Indian tribes first hunted them for meat but were quick to see the advantages given by the horse in war and hunting.

The American Saddlebred (*above*) is a five-gaited horse now bred almost exclusively for the show ring. His bearing is outstanding and the very high arched head carriage is characteristic as is the high tail carriage.

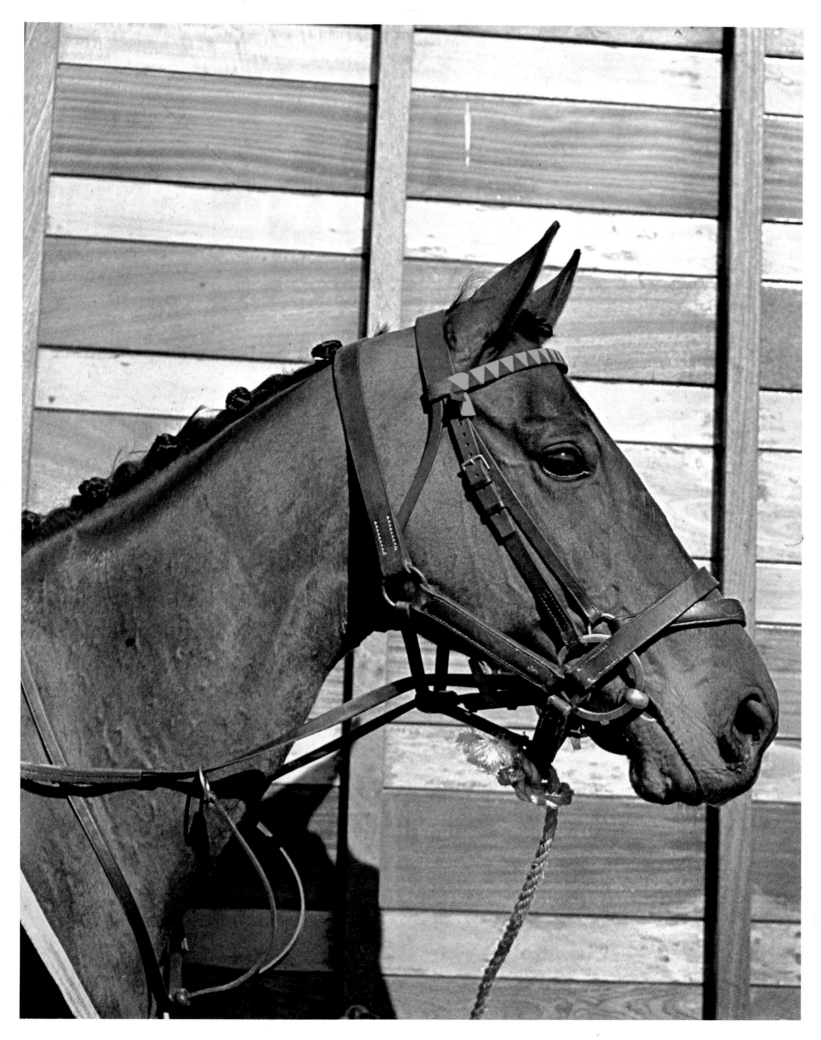

MARES AND FOALS

When a favourite mare has fulfilled her purpose as a riding and working animal, nothing brings more pleasure than to breed from her. The sight of a new-born foal playing happily in one's own paddock can bring endless fun and pride both to the owner and the mare. Foals are amongst the most independent of any young animals and two or three days after birth they are sure to be found investigating all sorts of strange objects and exploring new places alone. They are born comics and will provide rewarding and amusing results for anyone equipped with a camera.

The breeding of a foal can be a most rewarding as well as time-consuming experience. Often if a mare sustains an injury which renders her useless for ridden work the answer is to put her into foal. Choosing a suitable stallion can be difficult but the Hunters Improvement Society has done a tremendous amount of work through their Premium Scheme to encourage the use of a quality stallion at a reasonable stud fee.

The mare will carry her foal for eleven months before birth and within minutes after it is born the foal will attempt to get to its feet and take its first wobbly, unsteady steps. Somehow there always seems to be far too much leg for the foal to cope with during the first few hours and he will frequently fall over his own ungainly legs. However, he rapidly learns how to get them under control and is soon leaping around the paddock with all the gay abandon of any young animal in a new world. Mares and foals are often all turned out together in order to encourage the youngsters to play with each other and develop their limbs by racing round the field. It is a legacy from the days when horses were subject to the dangers of predatory animals that enables the young foal to become mobile in such a short space of time. When part of a herd of wild ponies, it was essential that both mare and foal should be able to move off with the herd as soon as danger threatened.

The countless wild native ponies of Britain foal quite naturally on the wide open expanse of their native Exmoor and Dartmoor, or in the New Forest, as do the wild horses of Wyoming in North America, but the more valuable thoroughbred mares and breeding stock are kept under constant watch on the stud farms. Some establishments even have close circuit television. Mares are sensitive about foaling in the presence of human beings and some will refuse to foal unless left alone.

A young foal (*left*) has—literally—to stand on its own four feet as soon as possible after its birth for, like all young and defenceless animals which rely upon the protection of the rest of the herd, a horse born in the wild would be very vulnerable to any predator if it could not keep up with the other horses.

Under natural conditions in the wild a foal would probably not have been fully weaned until its mother got tired of it and it would have stayed with the herd until chased off by the stallion. It might then lead a solitary life or join up with a band of other young bachelors until it was older and strong enough to challenge an adult for the leadership of another herd. In the domestic horse weaning is usually controlled by man and although mother and foal have a close bond for the first few months of the young horse's life (*right*) this is broken when they are deliberately separated at about six months old. With most horses they then have another three years or more in which to mature before being broken in but racehorses, especially in America, are often broken in much earlier and even raced before they are two years old. This is possible because however demanding racing may prove it does not require a wide range of activities or learning on the horse's part.

The chestnut Thoroughbred foal makes the first advances and after a little difficulty wins the confidence of the shy and delicate Arab. Thereafter the two are inseparable . . . though it is still the chestnut who takes the lead.

A roan pony and her Palomino foal (*right*) seemingly ripe for mischief. Roans are ponies that have white hairs mixed fairly evenly with hairs of another colour—bay, black or chestnut, and the coat often has a bluish tinge to it. Like Palominos, roans are a colouring and do not constitute a breed.

The Shire is essentially a heavily built working horse and this foal (*left*) has travelled to a show with his mother. The bustle and hurry of a big show is obviously too much for such a little chap and he has settled himself next to the horsebox for a nap.

A new-born foal takes some hours to get steady on his legs. This New Forest pony (*below*) has not yet learned to stand.

A beautifully marked Skewbald mare and her sturdy foal (*right*), though his legs still splay out in the typical manner of the very young. Skewbald is a pattern, known in America as Paint, and not a breed. The particolour effect is frequently in red and white as here.

Foals can be very frisky but, like all young animals, need plenty of rest (*left*). In natural conditions they will continue to suckle from their mothers (*below*) until such time as her milk dries up. In artificial conditions created by man, a foal can be weaned at any time after four and a half months. A two-week-old foal will begin to nibble at the grass and as soon as this is noticed attempts can be made to encourage the foal to eat concentrates. Youngsters are usually broken to halter (*right*) between the ages of three and five years but Thoroughbreds destined for the racecourse may be broken much earlier. Horses are considered foals up to the January following their birth—almost nine months.

THE RACE HORSE

'The sport of kings and the king of sports'—so the greatest of all forms of equine sport has been aptly described. As long as man is connected with horses he will always strive to prove that his horse is superior to that of his neighbour. The ultimate deciding factor must always be the speed and stamina of the respective horses. Since the earliest times, when speed was a necessity to escape from one's enemies, tremendous value has been placed on the ability to move faster than anybody else for very obvious reasons. Since the eighteenth century the specialized and selective breeding of Thoroughbreds has produced a succession of near perfect specimens of the horse, which have been capable of out-distancing all their rivals. In the history of racing on both sides of the Atlantic the names and records of Eclipse, St Simon and Hyperion in England and Sir Archy, Peytona, Fashion and Longfellow in America live on beside the names of today such as Kelso, the leading money winner in history, Nearco, Nijinsky and Mill Reef, to name just a few. Very few horses have unbeaten records but Ribot, the legendary Italian horse, has this distinction. He won the Prix de l'Arc de Triomphe twice, and it is one of the most difficult races to win in the world. The fact that he managed this is a measure of his greatness.

The racing scene, whether it is Derby Day in England, Cup Day in Melbourne, the Durban July or the Kentucky Derby, attracts a colourful, noisy and essentially happy crowd of enthusiasts. Celebrities and the unknown public jostle noisily together around the parade paddock, assessing the chances of the runners, and many people (in particular the owners and trainers) know that vast sums of money are going to be won or lost in the next ten minutes. The bell rings and the jockeys mount to proceed down to the start. Starting stalls are now in use almost everywhere in the world and ensure the fairest possible beginning to any race. With a cry of 'They're off', the fluid blaze of colour sets out at a cracking pace. Excitement mounts as the horses separate, then the finishing post draws nearer and nearer, binoculars are trained on the leaders, the commentator engenders more excitement with every word and suddenly it is all over and the winner of yet another contest is led amidst the cheering crowds to the winner's enclosure. Proud owners and trainers make their way to congratulate horse and jockey. The lucky punters collect their winnings, the losers resolve never to trust their money to a four-legged friend ever again, but sure enough they are the first to lay bets on the next race! The scene is the same the world over wherever horses are produced to race against each other. Whether on the flat or over the sticks, the excitement is the same, from the local point-to-point to the Classics. Many thousands of pounds can be won with a successful racehorse, but even more revenue can be secured when a successful horse is retired to stud. Other owners, all anxious to obtain some of the characteristics of a really top-class horse, will pay vast sums for a nomination for their mares to the best stallion in the world. Yearlings such as Vaguely Noble and Crowned Prince then fetch record prices at the Yearling Sales purely on the merits of their breeding and the hoped-for racing results. Some of the most successful horses on the track may not have hit the highest price bracket at Newmarket, but can turn up trumps in the final reckoning.

There are a vast number of racing enthusiasts who are not often present on the course except at their nearest meeting—radio and television have brought thousands of fans and have made certain horses and the places associated with them everyday household words. Names like Longchamps—home of the French classic race, Le Prix de l'Arc de Triomphe; Epsom, where the Derby, the blue riband of the racing world, is run every year in June; Aintree, home of the world's greatest steeplechase; Aqueduct on Long Island, New York, and Churchill Downs, and finally Kentucky, venue for the great Kentucky Derby, are all well known to many millions of people. Similarly, names of horses come to the fore through the mass media. Ribot and Man o'War, Nijinsky and Arkle are names that crop up time and again. These horses have become idols in their time, so popular that people will pay ridiculous sums for shoes worn by the horse in question. Eventually the popularity of some reach pop-star proportions and they have to be protected from their fans, who are often keen to obtain souvenirs, such as hairs from their favourite's tail.

Statues are erected in memory of these great horses. Hyperion and Chamossaire stand for ever at the centre of English racing, and their life-size models are to be seen at Newmarket, while Gladiateur guards the entrance to Longchamps. Similarly Man o'War lives on at Fayette County near Lexington in the heart of American racing country, Kentucky. China models are cast of the top favourites, pictures are painted and reproduced in

The much loved Arkle (*right*), only unplaced once in seventy races, thirty-five of which he won, proved himself beyond all doubt to be a truly great steeplechaser. After a tragic accident in 1966 when he broke his pedal bone, his owner and trainer waited almost two years to see if he would run again. Courageously, his owner took the unenviable decision that Arkle should never race again. This was a truly great horse with an unquenchable spirit and a desire to win at all costs. He loved the admiration of his followers and was a tremendous showman whenever he appeared in public.

thousands for the fans. You can now decorate your home with portraits of Mill Reef, Golden Miller and Sir Ivor; or with a porcelain model of your favourite steeple-chaser, flat racer or show jumper. Racing in England takes place on the springy green turf as it does in Australia, but this is not always the case in other parts of the world. Aqueduct has a dirt track, Laurel Park has both grass and dirt tracks though in the main racing in America takes place on dirt tracks.

It is not only the horses and places that become house-hold names—jockeys and trainers are equally popular, such as the legendary Fred Archer, or Sir Gordon Richards, now a highly successful trainer, or Scobie Breasley, an Australian who did much of his race-riding in Britain. Others are Lester Piggot, who still stands un-rivalled at the top of his profession, Yves Saint Martin, Eddie Arcaro and William Shoemaker of America. And don't forget the steeplechase jockeys, Arkle's partner,

Pat Taafe, and Tommy Smith who came to England with Jay Trump from America and won the Grand National in 1965. Then there is Fred Winter, who won the French steeplechase on Mandarin with a broken bit, his only remaining control being the reins round the horse's neck.

These and many more are given film star treatment during their careers, but it is not all glamour. They have all worked long and hard and patiently to perfect their skill and that of their horses and have often had to wait for their successes. There is also a great deal of effort put in behind the scenes by the faithful stable lads and grooms, which goes unnoticed by the general public, but which is essential to any success. And the horses work hard too—the immortal Arkle won over £75,000 for his owner, having cost 1,150 guineas as a youngster at the Dublin Sales. But to win this huge sum steeple-chasing, Arkle had to gallop almost 100 miles and jump

Steeplechasing is probably the most exciting, and most dangerous, of all horse sports. It requires great skill and absolute confidence on the part of horse and jockey. The last fence negotiated (*left*), the horses still have to fight it out in the final stretch of flat.

Spanish Steps (*right*) takes a fence in the Gainsborough Chase at Sandown Park.

some 600 fences and hurdles. In contrast, a three-year-old colt in the Derby can earn nearly as much by running twelve furlongs on the flat and winning this English Classic.

The excitements of racing are by no means limited to the flat and the steeplechase. There are all kinds of driving races: scurry racing, hackney carriage, four-in-hand and chuck wagon racing in true Wild West style, but the main rival to the jockey's race is trotting racing which enjoys great popularity in North America, Australia and many other countries.

In many continental countries, Germany, Italy, Finland and Scandinavia, and particularly in Holland where the sport began, trotters and pacers are held in as high esteem as flat racing and steeplechasing horses — and sometimes higher. In France this form of racing started in 1836, and of the many thousands of trotting horses now registered in that country the majority are Noram Trotters, or Demi-Sangs which are raced under saddle as well as in harness. The old sport of harness racing was once very popular in the North of England, but although it is being revived to some extent, the British racing trotter has little prestige compared with its European counterpart. Russia's well-known breed, the Orlov-Trotter, was crossed with the American Standardbred to produce the comparatively new and very fast Métis Trotter. With the North Swedish Trotter, Sweden has the distinction of possessing the only 'cold-blood' horse of this category in the world.

Harness racing is a hot favourite in New Zealand and Australia, and both countries have produced trotting and pacing speed records to vie with, and in some cases surpass, those of America. Meetings are often held at night on floodlit tracks, and it was this innovation that really popularized the sport, just as it did in Canada and America.

Some racehorses wear blinkers to prevent their being distracted during the race (*above*). This pair has just taken a jump in the Langley Handicap Hurdle Race at Windsor.

The Grand National course at Aintree is one of the most gruelling in the world (*left*). Any horse that runs in this race has to be supremely strong and fit to survive. Here the field takes the water jump.

Australia is one of the most successful racing nations in the world and several speed records have been set up at the Randlewick Racecourse in Sydney. In the Northern Territory the course at Brunette Downs is a sandy track presenting a very different picture from the English racing scene on green turf (*right*). Here horses set out from the paddock at the start of a race.

The great Nijinsky (*right*), one of the outstanding horses of the 1970s, and maybe of all time. This Canadian-bred, Irish-trained colt caught the public's imagination with his star-like quality during his racing career. Only the twelfth horse in 161 years to win the 'Triple Crown', which includes the 2000 guineas, the Derby and the St Leger, Nijinsky's ancestry can be traced back to one of the all-time greats in the racing world—Lord Derby's Hyperion. Ridden by champion jockey, Lester Piggot, he is seen here returning to the winner's enclosure at Ascot after his victory in the King George VI and Queen Elizabeth Stakes.

The ten minutes before a race are often more important than the race itself, as those who have backed a horse anxiously watch to see if their favourite is looking fit, or to examine the going and study the changing odds. One's earlier decision to back a horse which has been based on breeding, form and the jockey booked to ride may suddenly be reversed as one sees the rest of the field walking round the paddock. The jockeys mount and positively the last chance to judge the animals and change one's mind is when they canter down to the start (*left*). Here Tribal Chief and Joe Mercer go down to the start at Windsor Great Park.

Racing colours, stylish-looking jockeys and impressive grandstands might be seen on racecourses in any part of the world but a racehorse with a magnificent mane (*centre left*) is not likely to be seen in Western Europe or America. This fine horse is an Arab photographed on the course at Warsaw. Although Arabs are largely kept for beauty and breeding, rather than for racing, Arab races are still held in Poland and some parts of the Soviet Union where meetings, complete with tote, are attended by enthusiastic crowds.

Colourful parades before the race are a popular and eye-catching feature of American racetracks (*below left*). The runners are escorted to the post by red-jacket outriders and grooms as in this post parade at Aqueduct, the racecourse on Long Island.

The Royal Ascot meeting (*right*) is one of the most popular in Britain and women who go to the members enclosure are notorious for vying with each other over the size, colour and brilliance of their hats. For the masses packing the stands interest is concentrated on the equally gaily-coloured field.

Epsom is an equally famous British course and the left-handed Tattenham Corner (*centre right*), on a steep slope has a strong influence on the result of a race.

Modern race jockeys owe their inheritance of the 'crouch' seat (*below right*) to James Todhunter Sloan ('Tod Sloan'). He was an American jockey who in 1897 brought the now familiar forward seat from America to the British Isles. He showed that by crouching forward with very short leathers, wind-resistance could be reduced and a faster speed would therefore result. These jockeys are fighting out a close finish as the end wire comes up at Aqueduct.

Women riders made their first appearance in the history of the British Turf when the Jockey Club permitted twelve experimental ladies' flat races in 1972. The prejudice against lady jockeys had been swept away a few years earlier in the United States. Miss Meriel Tufnell (*left*) became the first lady champion rider. She won the inaugural race at Kempton Park on her mother's Scorched Earth and had gained the most points by the end of the season.

Mill Reef (*above*), photographed here with Geoff Lewis up, was the outstanding racehorse of 1971. Owned by Paul Mellon, he won the Eclipse stakes, the Derby, the Prix de l'Arc de Triomphe and the King George VI and Queen Elizabeth Stakes.

Trotting racing (*above*) is extremely popular in America, Australia and the Soviet Union but it has never caught on in Britain. It demands considerable skill for the lightweight cart can easily be overturned if a driver tries to take a corner too tightly.

Chuck wagon racing (*below*), an exciting reminder of the days of the Old West, provides plenty of thrills in North America. The wagons are stripped down for speed. Controlling the wagon team and avoiding a spill or a collision is a test of the most experienced driver.

SHOW JUMPING AND EVENTING

Show jumping is today a very popular sport in both the United States and Europe and interest is growing increasingly in South Africa, Canada and Australia. Combined training for the three disciplines of dressage, cross country and show jumping is also attracting more and more attention. Standards in show jumping are now so high that both horse and rider must be specialists and only a few riders can afford the expense in both time and money to compete at the higher levels so that this is becoming a field for the professional. Eventing demands an all-round horse which can manage the dressage, a gruelling twenty-mile endurance test of a cross country course with thirty big fences and a small and twisting show-jumping course. Even at top level this is still an amateur affair.

In England the heroes and heroines of international arenas are known to most people, and the more famous of their horses have huge numbers of fans. In the last fifteen years television has been responsible for turning the riders and their horses into stars and for the interest taken in the many different shows all over the world which culminate in the four-yearly Olympics; but it was the members of the BSJA in the years immediately after the war that were responsible for building up the British team to a standard comparable with that of the continental teams so that their successes aroused the interest of the general public. The names of the fifties are still as well known as those of today: Colonel Sir Mike Ansell, who was the leading light of the BSJA and organizer of the Royal International Horse Show at the White City in 1947, of the Horse of the Year Show at Harringay and also the British team's excellence abroad; Colonel Harry Llewellyn and the great Foxhunter who are show jumping's heroes; Pat Smythe with Prince Hal and Tosca; Peter Robeson and Craven A, and Wilf White and Nizefela.

Since then the numbers of riders and of shows, both national and international, have grown considerably. Douglas Bunn started the All-England Jumping Ground at Hickstead in 1960 which now rivals the great continental showgrounds like Aachen, Hamburg and Rotterdam. Many more women are now among the stars and they have their own World and European Championships and the coveted Queen Elizabeth II Cup at the Royal International Horse Show, which is as prized as the King George V Cup for men. Alison Westwood and The Maverick, Anneli Drummond-Hay and Merely-a-Monarch, Marion Mould and the amazing little pony, Stroller, and Anne Moore and Psalm have all made show jumping the exciting, dramatic and popular sport that it is now. Fine riders such as Lucinda Prior-Palmer and H.R.H. the Princess Anne, who carried off both First and Second prizes in the European Three Day competition at Luhmühlen in 1975, have contributed to the high standard in eventing. Among the men names like Alan Oliver, Harvey Smith and David Broome, European Champion three times running and World Show Jumping Champion from 1970-74, head Britain's top-class riders while Britain's Olympic team carried off the Eventing Gold Medals at both Mexico in 1968 and Munich in 1972.

The United States Olympic team was reorganized after the war under the successive captaincies of Colonel John Woffard, Arthur MacCashin and Bill Steinkraus who took over in 1955 and was individual Gold Medallist on Snowbound at the Mexico Olympics in 1968. The team has been a formidable one for many years and one which has been reckoned as the most stylish in the world —principally from the time that Bertalan de Nemethy was appointed trainer just before the Stockholm Olympics. Since then their team has done consistently well in Nations Cups and individual events in Europe and England as well as in America. They have won the President's Cup twice since its inauguration in 1965 and in 1972 carried off a silver medal at the Olympics as they did at Rome in 1960. The new World Show Jumping Champion is an American, Bruce Davidson, who is only in his early twenties. North America's three important shows are at New York, Harrisburg and Toronto, together with the Pan American Games.

The European countries have produced famous riders, horses and teams consistently, many of whom have been winning for the last twenty years. Hans Winkler from Germany and his courageous little mare Halla are always remembered for their remarkable performance at the Stockholm Olympics, when Winkler had injured himself before the final round and went into jump barely able to stay in the saddle because of the pain. Halla virtually took herself around the enormous course and had a clear round to win both the individual Gold Medal and the Team Gold for Germany. Alvin Schockemohle, who carried off the Grand Prix at the Royal International Horse Show in 1975, on Rex the Robber, his brother Paul, and Hartwig Steenken, Men's Champion in 1974 on his mare Simone, are other leading German riders. They have twice won the President's Cup and four times the Prix des Nations, the Olympic's most prestigious award.

Mary Chapot on White Lightening (*right*) jumping at Hickstead in 1968, the year they won the Queen Elizabeth II Cup at the Royal International Horse Show. Later that year she took the place of Steinkraus in the American team at the Mexico Olympics as his horse Snowbound had lamed himself in the Individual event.

There are two main reasons for the dominance of the German team. Their horses are immensely powerful and they have a comparatively phlegmatic temperament that makes them accept a rigorous training system which would be resented by high-couraged animals with more thoroughbred blood in them. Instant obedience and utter submissiveness are the keynotes, and though both qualities are desirable to some extent, taken too far they rob the horse of his initiative and, if things go wrong, he is unable to assist.

There are many other riders who are internationally known. Pierre Jonqueres d'Oriola from France with various horses such as Ali Baba, Lutteur and Pomona has been winning since 1947, the d'Inzeo brothers from Italy have between them over the last two decades won every major honour several times over, and Nelson Pessoa, the great Brazilian show jumper and his famous horse Gran Geste are all among the celebrated members of this sport.

In 1958 the first and only team from South Africa came to Europe and competed successfully, but since about 1960 the horse sickness ban has been in force and prevented riders from South Africa from bringing their own horses or competing in teams outside their own country. However, South African riders have come to Europe and Bob Grayston, Mickey Louw and Gonda Butters are well known outside their own country. In 1970 the indoor show at Johannesburg had a world class touch as Broome, Pessoa, d'Oriola and Schridde all went over to compete against the locals. In Australia and New Zealand there is a lively interest, though the teams are limited by the enormous distances they have to travel to compete against anyone else other than each other. However the Australians won an Olympic Gold Medal in Rome and in the year of the Tokyo Olympics they made a grand tour of Europe after the games during their quarantine period.

Some of the world's top show jumpers change hands for very considerable sums of money so it is not hard to imagine how such a valuable charge is cared for. But to reach this class it has not always been easy for horse and rider. Much hard work goes on behind the scenes before

Harvey Smith (*far left*) and David Broome (*left*), two of Britain's best known show jumping riders, have opted for professional status which makes them ineligible to represent their country in the Olympics. Both have previously been in Olympic teams and David Broome has twice won personal bronze medals in the Games. Harvey Smith, here riding his horse Archie at Hickstead in 1971, is a skilled horseman, popular with the large public which follows show jumping today, who has few rivals while David Broome has been three times the European Champion and the World Show Jumping Champion from 1970–74. Seen here riding Manhattan (now called Jaegermeister), which has recently done exceedingly well in the United States, he has always had a string of first-class ponies and horses with which he has been incredibly successful.

Anneli Drummond-Hay and her horse Monarch (*right*) began their career in three-day eventing and have won both the Badminton and Burghley horse trials. They later switched to show jumping and are seen here taking a jump at Hickstead in 1971, the year that Anneli achieved her ambition to win the coveted Queen Elizabeth II Cup at the Royal International Horse Show. Monarch is a horse with that indefinable star quality that attracts vast crowds to see him jump.

a top-class jumper or eventer is produced. And it is the same for the show horses—ponies, hacks, hackneys and hunters all have to undergo a thorough training period before they are ready to appear in the arena. The road is long and hard but the rewards at the top are worth every minute of the battle to get there. The feeling of pride as the champion rosette is pinned to your horse's bridle, and your lap of honour is applauded by the admiring crowd seems to make the work and effort all worthwhile. But it is not only the winning that counts, and it is just as pleasing to many people to produce a horse capable of going well in the hunting field or across country. A great deal of personal satisfaction can be gained by the good performance of your horse as a result of patient work beforehand whether he wins or not. It is extremely rare for the experience of working and living with horses to be unrewarding and they are capable of deep friendships and trust as well as great things in the arena. There are many dedicated workers behind the international show jumping scene who never appear in front of the television cameras but without whom no

show jumper could exist. A great deal of work is involved in the keeping of valuable animals that work hard, and a professional rider does not have the time to do the half of it, so it is the grooms and people backstage as well as the riders and their horses who are responsible for the thrills of an international competition.

This is true, of course, for every horse whose rider does not look after it totally on his own. Whenever you are admiring the turnout at a show, or at a meeting of the local hunt, or maybe a polo match, spare a thought for the work that goes on behind the scenes in order to produce the supremely fit and well-trained animals that you are privileged to watch. There are countless grooms who devote their lives to the welfare of the horses in their charge and often spend all their time tending to a sick or injured animal when they should be off-duty or catching up on their sleep. Girls who are employed in the big hunting stables begin their day at crack of dawn to prepare their charges and then have to cope with dirty and exhausted horses when they return at night after an arduous day's hunting.

47

Nelson Pessoa (*above*), the brilliant Brazilian rider, has had to campaign in Europe as the lone representative of his country. He bases himself in Chantilly and competes regularly all over the continent. He has won the marathon Hickstead Derby on two occasions on his brilliant little grey, Gran Geste. He also won the men's European Show Jumping Championship at Lucerne in 1966. He has the enviable and possibly unrepeatable record of having won the gigantic Hamburg Derby on no less than four occasions on Gran Geste.

Captain of the USA show jumping team, and one of the prime architects of the American team's rise to prominence, Bill Steinkraus (*above left*) is an old campaigner in the show jumping ring. He won the individual Gold Medal at the Olympics in Mexico in 1968 on Snowbound. He is riding Fleet Apple, here, in the Nations Cup at Hickstead in 1971.

Marion Coakes (now Mrs Mould) caught the public's imagination on her horse Stroller (*right*). When she persuaded her father to let her keep her pony to use in adult classes she was proved phenomenally right for he has a fantastic record both at home and abroad and is an individual Olympic Silver Medal winner.

Cross country courses contain a wide variety of fences built up and down hill to test the stamina, skill and courage of both horse and rider (*left*). Here a fine grey Irish horse and his rider take a drop fence in their stride.

The beautiful style of riding of Anneli Drummond-Hay (*left*) is clear for all to see and her horses are impeccably schooled and capable of performing in the dressage arena. She achieved a great double in 1969 when she won both the Hickstead Derby and the equivalent in Rome. This time her success was gained on her bouncy ex-hunt servant's horse, Xanthos. Seen here riding Sporting Ford at Hickstead in 1971 she was European Ladies Champion in 1968 and has proved her ability as a top lady rider—one of the most stylish of them all.

H.R.H. Princess Anne (*right*) and her husband Captain Mark Phillips (*below left*) are active participants in all show events: dressage, cross country and show jumping. Captain Phillips, who was a member of the British Olympic team at Munich, is seen here during the Badminton Horse Trials of 1971 at which he was the victor, a success he repeated at the Trials of 1974 riding Columbus, a strapping grey which had proved a little too strong for the Princess.

Princess Anne was herself victor in the Burghley three-day event in 1971 on Doublet, a horse bred by Her Majesty the Queen and entirely produced by Princess Anne and her trainer Alison Oliver. It must have given her mother great pleasure to present her with the trophy for the Individual European Championship. She is seen here on Doublet in the show jumping, which forms the final phase of the Three Day Trials, to prove that after the rigours of the previous day's speed and endurance test and cross country course, the horse is still obedient and supple enough to complete a show jumping course.

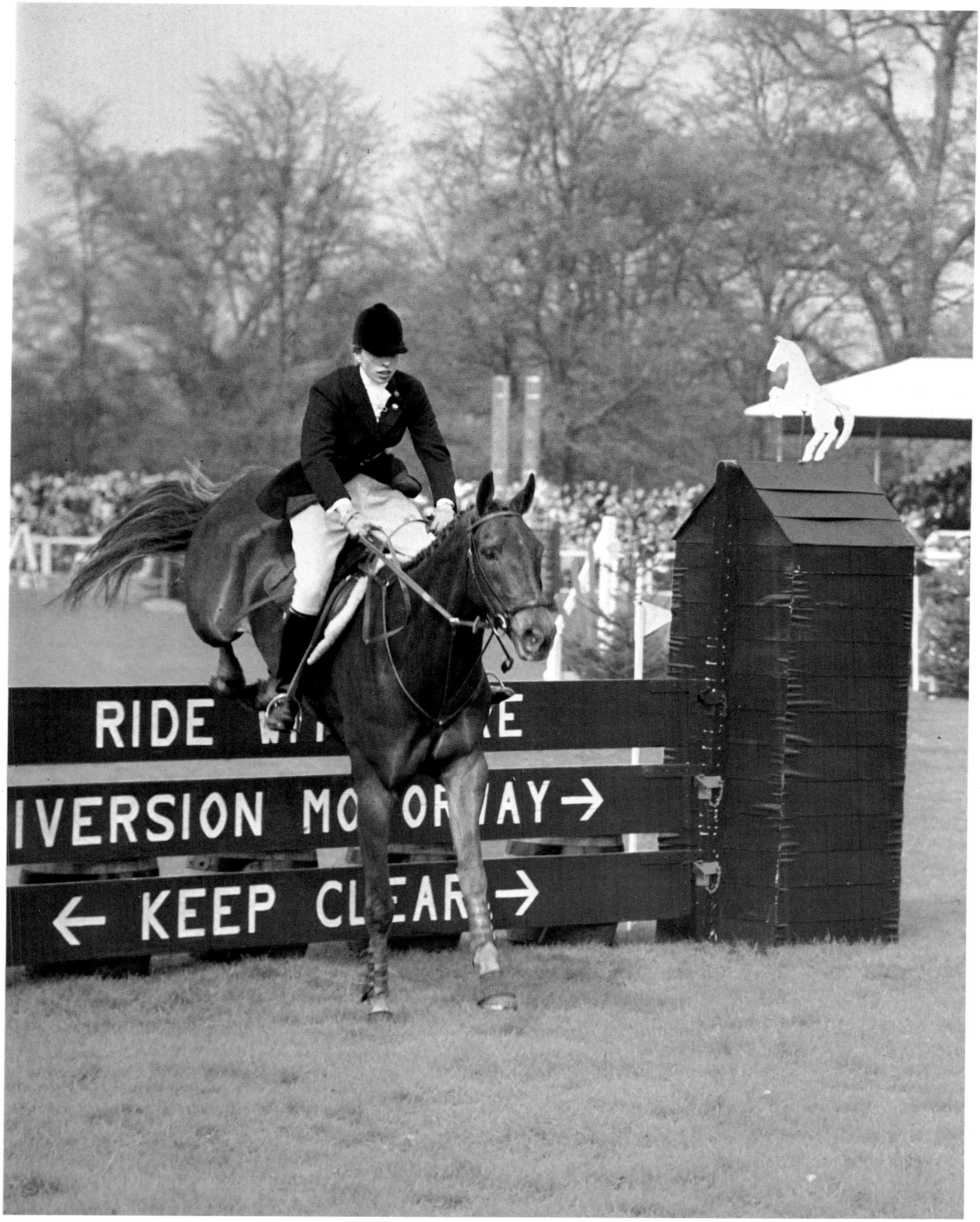
RIDE
IVERSION
KEEP

ON PARADE

Whenever there is a procession or a parade, an occasion of splendour and ritual, the horse has had a traditional role, carrying the hero, drawing the state carriage. Outriders and cavalry have added dignity and spectacle and dazzling horses, colourful uniforms and the pageantry of the years have brought glamour to the occasion. Show jumpers, three-day eventers, world class polo ponies, hunt horses, show ponies, rodeo ponies, circus performers and many more excite the crowds they attract and demand acknowledgement of their skill but it is the ceremonial horse that receives the greatest admiration from the public.

Some, like the horses of the Canadian Mounted Police and various other police forces, have an everyday working job to do. They are quite indispensable in some situations, such as crowd control, when no machine could do their job but it is when leading a parade or putting on a special display to show their skill and training to the public that they come into their own.

Even the heavy horse has his moment, not just at the agricultural shows and in ploughing competitions but on occasions like the Horse of the Year Show in London when you can see the magnificent sight of six teams of heavy horses harrowing the arena during their majestic musical drive.

But none of these is as impressive or as beautiful as the proud horses which draw a royal coach or escort a head of state on an official visit, or stand guard outside a royal palace.

In London the Royal Mews behind Buckingham Palace is open to the visitor and every day in London's streets you can see the troops of the Household Cavalry on duty. In Sweden, Denmark and Iran the royal stables are still maintained in Stockholm, Copenhagen and Teheran and many other countries still maintain a ceremonial cavalry escort. Even in communist Czechoslovakia the president may travel in the official state carriage drawn by a fine team of six handsome Kladruber greys.

At Saumur, on the Loire, France still maintains the Cavalry School founded by Napoleon where they keep up the tradition of the *Haute Ecole*, the classic equestrian skills which are echoed in modern dressage events. Their light and gay performances, precise movements accurately carried out by riders dressed in uniforms of purple and gold are a delight to watch. But even they cannot match the magnificence of the performers at the Spanish Riding School.

The Spanish Riding School is not in Spain but in Vienna, and is named for its horses which are of Spanish origin. It is older than Saumur and was founded early in the eighteenth century by the Emperor Charles VI, and modelled on the great Riding Academy of Versailles (disbanded during the French Revolution). The School is renowned for having the most highly skilled riders and most perfectly trained horses in the world and their displays are deservedly famous.

The School's grey Lippizaner stallions are perhaps the most impressive and beautiful horses in the world. Their name comes from Lippiza, a small village on the Adriatic coast which once belonged to Austria and where, until the First World War, the horses used exclusively by the Riding School were bred. Today these horses of great beauty, intelligence and stamina are bred at a stud in Piber, Austria. They all come from five families. It is only the grey Lipizzaner stallions which perform the controlled movements of *Haute Ecole* at the Spanish Riding School. They are all born black, and turn grey and finally white as they grow older, but there are also bay and chestnut horses in the breed.

The different strains vary in type, and in height from 14 to 16 hands, but all make excellent carriage horses as well as riding horses—Lipizzaners were chosen and specially imported to Iran to draw the Shahanshah's Coronation Coach in 1967, and when all decked out in ceremonial harness were a truly magnificent sight.

The Piber stud's grey stallions are taken for a long and complex training, which begins after years of very careful breaking in and the normal training that most good riding horses undergo. They then learn all the special manoeuvres for which they are famous: the Volte, which is the execution of very small circles; the Pesade, a turn on the haunches; Levade, Piaffe, Passage and so on. Perhaps the most spectacular is the Capriole when the horse springs high in the air and then when he reaches his highest point kicks out horizontally with his hind legs so that it seems as if he is flying.

In the hall of the Riding School are two upright posts about four feet apart. Between these the horse is loosely tethered while taught some of his manoeuvres, first without, then with a rider before being allowed to perform away from the pillars.

The riders of the Spanish Riding School go through just as rigorous a training as their mounts and it will be several years before they are allowed to appear before the public. It is not easy to maintain the standards of the finest equestrianism in the world.

The Royal Horse Guards (*right*), together with the Life Guards make up the Household Cavalry of the British Army. They are also known as 'The Blues' from their tunic colour which, with their red plumes and black sheepskins on their saddles, differentiate them from their Life Guard colleagues. Since their amalgamation with the Royal Dragoons they are now more often known as the 'Blues and Royals'.

'The horse first, and then yourself.' One of the Canadian 'Mounties' (Royal Canadian Mounted Police) puts the finishing touches to his equipment after he has prepared his mount before going on parade (*left*). Established in 1871 to help settle the west, they are still famous for their wonderful mounted musical rides.

A troop of Life Guards (*right*) cross Horse Guard's Parade. The Household Cavalry's mounts are all black horses selected from three- and four-year-old Irish stock except for those of the State Trumpeters, which are greys, and the drum horses (*below*) which are piebald or skewbald. The drum horses have to be exceptionally strong to carry the weight of the huge drums for long periods. The gold state uniform and velvet caps, originating in the time of Charles II, are worn only in the presence of royalty. The horses are trained to respond to the directions of the reins controlled from the stirrup irons, so that the riders can keep their hands free for their drum-sticks. During the summer the Household Cavalry journeys down to Pirbright in Surrey for a period under canvas exchanging soft turf for the hard London streets. Troop horses also compete in show jumping and eventing during the summer.

The riders and magnificent Lippizaner stallions of the Spanish Riding School in Vienna present spectacular displays in the ring of the riding school which adjoins the Imperial Palace. Entering the ring for the Quadrille (*left*) they are dressed in their traditional uniform of black bicorn, tail coat, dazzling white breeches and shining top boots. They salute the portrait of their founder and then sometimes ride in single file right into the main visitors' box and canter round the somewhat startled guests in a tight circle before starting the display.

Their magnificent display of horsemanship includes both intricate steps and complicated manoeuvres both singly and in formation. One of the most moving and beautifully controlled sequences consists of the horses moving across each other in diagonal lines in the stately Spanish Trot (*above*). The Passage (*right*) is a development of the Piaffe, a slow-moving gait performed on the spot without advancing, retiring or moving to the side, in which the legs are gracefully raised high and flexed. In the Passage a slow, regular and very dignified movement forward is allowed. It is one of the basic gaits of equestrianism which can still be seen performed by experts in Britain and elsewhere.

The precise training of these beautiful white horses and the fine horsemanship of their riders set off by the baroque splendours of the architecture of the Riding School must be an inspiration to anyone who has the chance to see them.

Among the 'airs above the ground' performed by the horses of the Spanish Riding School is the Pesade (*previous pages, left*), in which the horse lifts its forelegs off the ground on one spot without moving forward, keeping the hind legs on the ground without moving them so that he does not keep time with his hind legs. It is first learned on loose reins with no rider. It was originally designed to prepare a horse for leaping with greater freedom and to gain control of his forelegs.

The Courbette (*previous pages, right*), a movement which was once most valuable in battle, is a leap in which the horse goes up higher in front, balancing on its hind legs with deeply bent hocks and then brings the hind legs forward in a low but smart action, in concert with the forelegs at the moment when they come to the ground.

A parade does not always have to be a staged event. Sometimes parade and spectators are all one. For instance, in the Spanish town of Seville one week in the spring is given over to the famous Seville April Fair, at which business is essentially still the selling and buying of horses. Fiesta time is the signal for the handsome horsemen to parade along the streets of Seville on their beautiful Carthusian and Arab horses, sometimes unaccompanied, and at other times carrying girls dressed in their exquisite dresses a crupa behind them (*below*). With the gaily decorated streets, Seville offers one of the most splendid sights to be found anywhere in the world.

Foxhunting is still a very traditional and ritualized sport at which horse and rider are on show as much as in any show ring especially at the meet which precedes the hunt itself which is always an attractive scene and draws local spectators. The horses are always fit and well turned out, and usually excited at the thought of the chase ahead of them. The 'pink' coats of the huntsmen, like those of the Old Surrey and Burstow Hunt (*right*), and the shining leather and saddlery stand out above the shifting scene of people and hounds, which move like quicksilver around the whipper-in. It is estimated that 50,000 mounted followers hunt every week in Britain. Foxhunting is also extremely popular in America, mainly in Virginia where some fine packs (with a preponderance of English blood lines) are to be found. Where there is a shortage of foxes, or none at all, the hunt follows a drag, or man-made trail as a substitute. It is never quite the same as foxhunting, when the excitement enables one to jump further and faster than ever before. Once the hounds have found there is no stopping the field as they swallow up hedge after hedge, providing a thrilling sight to those who are clever enough to follow close behind them. Although the interest in shows and jumping has increased enormously all over the world during the last ten years, the excitement of jumping unknown obstacles at speed and in company cannot be equalled in the artificial atmosphere of the show jumping arena. Not even riding a cross country course at a Three Day Event can equal the devil-may-care attitude of the hunter in pursuit of his quarry. The hunting field provides the ideal schooling ground for a young horse, whether he is destined for the eventing world, show jumping or steeplechasing.

WORKING HORSES

Although in the present mechanized age working horses no longer form a part of the everyday scene for most of us, there are still many places where they are hard at work making a very real contribution to life and to the national economy. Whatever their job they give their service willingly and without complaint. What is more they are reliable, and work happily on, provided they are well kept and well fed. They demand very little and give their all in return.

Over the centuries the horse has been the major method of transport and communication until he was replaced by the internal combustion engine. Think of the Pony Express where letters were carried 1,900 miles in eight days across the American continent, or the mail coaches of eighteenth- and early nineteenth-century England, which were famous for their speed and reliability. Not only mail, but passengers would also travel by this method.

At the end of the nineteenth century there were some 300,000 horses working for their living in the London area, 15,000 of them acting as cab and carriage horses while the rest pulled trams, coal carts, brewers' drays, greengrocers' carts, railway vans and many others. Nowadays the horse population of London is approximately 5,000, the majority being kept for the pleasure of riding although included in this figure are police horses, costermonger ponies and ceremonial horses.

Many world breeds have a drop or two of Clydesdale, or of Shire or Suffolk blood in their veins, and these are some of the breeds of big powerful horses that were essential to agriculture and heavy draft until they were supplanted by mechanization. After World War II it seemed that heavy horses were a thing of the past, except for those still indispensable to a few continental countries, and the animals kept for showing. But interest is reviving and numbers are slowly increasing.

Some breweries find that heavy draft horses used to deliver beer in major cities are an excellent advertisement and more economical on short haul than using lorries. A very popular spectacle is London's Lord Mayor's Day, and since 1954 a brewery has supplied six splendid grey Shires to draw the four and a half ton Lord Mayor's Coach through the City streets. Some farmers find it good policy to supplement tractors with a horse team, mainly for carting feed and for use when soil and weather conditions preclude weighty machines. Although ploughing is now normally a province of the tractor, there are 'horses only' ploughing matches in England, and even a few farms left which are still entirely reliant on literal horse power.

American shows are well supported by the Heavy Horse breeders and the competition is keen. As in Britain the 'Heavies' are used for both publicity and work, big horses are still in demand for logging where forest conditions can immobilize mechanical labour, and they are also used for such pleasure occupations as sleigh-riding, hay-rides, trekking, and the pulling contests.

The British Shire, as befits his ancestry, is the largest, pure-bred horse in the world. A modern Shire can shift five tons with ease, and his enormous strength, stamina and docility were some of the qualities progressively stabilized and improved after the Shire Horse Society was formed in 1878. These horses are still being exported to some American states, but like the Suffolk are now less common the other side of the Atlantic than the Belgian, Percheron and Clydesdale.

The Suffolk Punch is an ancient breed which has always been noted for its good trot. In Elizabethan times strong 'punchy' short-legged horses, less handsome than the modern version but of similar type, were needed to draw the first cumbersome coaches along the rutted tracks of England. Nowadays these excellent workers, always coloured some shade of chestnut, are exported to the Argentine, Canada and to the U.S.A.

Scotland's heavy horse, the Clydesdale, originated in the Clyde valley during the eighteenth century, when native mares were crossed with Flemish stallions to give more weight. A little leggier than Shires, these horses have a free action that especially suits them to draft work. Introduced into America about 1879 Clydesdales were, and still are, used for general work, and like all the heavy breeds are sometimes cross bred with light horses to produce good heavy and middle-weight hunters and jumpers.

The Netherlands and France have always been heavy horse countries and remain so today to a larger extent than elsewhere. The Belgian Heavy Draft, the modern representative of the old Flemish horse, now provides seventy per cent of America's heavy horse population.

Percherons, another heavy breed especially prevalent in the U.S.A. and Canada, originated in the La Perche region of France. These attractive grey or black horses are valued for their hardiness, activity and good, gentle temperament.

They were first imported to America in 1839, though the Percheron Horse Society of America was not established until 1905. The breed is widely distributed and there are Percherons in both Australia and Russia,

Major and Violet (*right*), a fine pair of heavy horses still used to draw the plough. The day of the working horse is by no means past. Some farmers still find them an economic proposition and there are always places that a horse can work which a tractor cannot reach.

In some parts of England and Scotland horses are still used for ploughing every day on small hill farms and the competitions for team ploughing (*above*) are becoming increasingly popular at agricultural shows. This pair are competing at the Southern Counties Agricultural Show.

In Canada and Australia horses are still frequently used to haul timber down from the forests (*above left*). A heavy collar helps the working horse take most of the strain on his strong shoulders. The market for English heavy horses has widened in recent years due to the demand from North America.

The Fjord pony of Norway (*top right*) is bred as a working pony. A certain amount of Arab blood has made him more distinguished than many working pony breeds but his ancestors have been known in Scandinavia for centuries. The stockmen of Australian sheep farms prefer to use horses for mustering their flocks (*right*) and looking after their farms. Mounted he has a higher vantage point.

but they arrived in Britain only in 1918—after the thousands of pure- and half-bred animals, brought over to France from Canada, the U.S.A. and the Argentine for Army Transport with the British Expeditionary Force, had more than proved their worth. These horses are no longer common in Britain, but a few British-bred Percherons have recently been exported to introduce fresh blood into the Canadian and American studs.

Many thousands of horses all over the world also work for their living by providing riding lessons for those not lucky enough to have their own horse or pony. Countless riding schools and trekking centres cater for the needs of everybody wishing to ride, from the beginner to the more advanced pupil. Next time you go to your own riding school, just spare a thought for your hard-working mount, who has probably already done two or three hours' work with the promise of more to come. As he patiently carries you round and round the school or sets off on his all-too-familiar hour-long hack, remember how much pleasure he can give you and reward him by trying to become a thoughtful and patient rider.

The London Harness Horse Society
organizes a yearly parade in Regent's
Park when both light and heavy trade
turnouts gather and parade (*left*).
Nosebags enable the team to have their
rations without returning to stable
during the day.

Portuguese bullfighting horses are
trained for many years before being
allowed to enter the arena and do a skilled
job. A good horse is highly valued and is
certainly not the 'bull fodder' that the
poor horses in neighbouring Spanish bull
rings may become. They do not wear
protective padding but are decked out in
fine regalia (*below*). They must be
prepared to charge head-on at the bull,
only darting away at the last moment.

At one time working horses were an
everyday sight in city streets but dray
horses are now frequently seen only at
parades or drawing a wagon for
promotional purposes. Many fine
animals are still in work like this prize-
winning Shire at a county show (*right*).

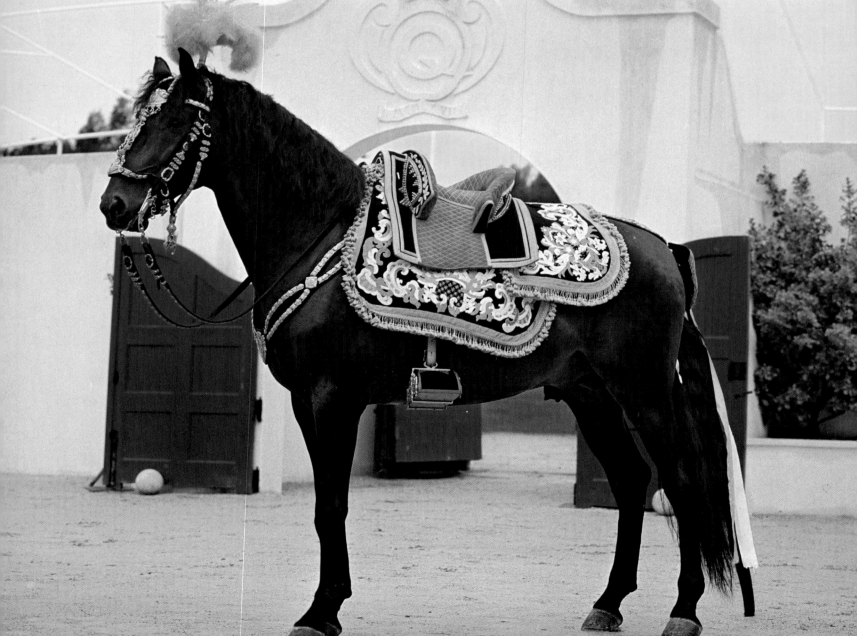

Although the days of the Wild West are no more, the huge ranches of North America still rely on the skills of the modern cowboy and the agility and knowledge of his horses. No jeep could deal with the unruly members of a beef herd like a cow pony (*left*) nor any machine sort the cattle into pens as effectively as this pair (*below*).

'Rodeo' is the Spanish for roundup and the rodeo was a natural development from the work of the Western cowboy. At first they were simply country fairs at which cowboys could show off their skill in riding and handling stock; today they also attract many professional bronco-busters. However, they still provide a place where the modern cowboy can compete against his fellow workers and show off his and his mount's skill. Roping calves, which forms a major part of his everyday work, is one of the many organized events (*top*). Complete co-ordination between horse and rider is essential if a calf is to be roped successfully. As soon as the lassoo has found its mark the horse will stop short and take the weight of the calf as the rope is firmly attached to the saddle. The cowboy then leaps to the ground and ties the calf securely. The other main events: bare-back riding, bull riding,

saddle bronc riding (*above right*) and steer wrestling (*above left*), in which the cowboy leaps dangerously from his horse to catch the steer when travelling at as much as 40 mph, all originate from the cowboy's everyday tasks on the ranch.

From the earliest days in the west, when two or three cowboys would bet on each other's skill in the main street of their home town, the rodeo has grown to the large-scale sport of today that can be seen all over the North American Continent. The professional riders can earn large sums of money and have attained a very high standard of skill and speed in all the events. The term rodeo did not come into use until the 1920s but the events were popular sports in the late nineteenth century.

Some of the biggest events attract visitors from all over the continent and overseas, who come to watch the cowboy pit his skills against his rival as well as against the broncs and bulls chosen to test his nerve and ability. The California Rodeo at Salinas runs for four days and includes a daily parade down Main Street of over 1,000 horses and riders all decked out in authentic

western costume. Ogden in Utah offers the thrills and spills of a pony express race and a goat-tying match. Cheyenne, as its name implies, boasts a tribal dance demonstration by Sioux Indians and a parade of horse-drawn vehicles unequalled anywhere in the world. But surely the crown must go to the ten-day Calgary Stampede which combines the usual attractions of rodeo with a food fair, an exhibition of livestock, commercial exhibits and square dancing in the streets. The Stampede Parade lasts about two hours in downtown Calgary as all the participants parade in their magnificent costumes.

In bronc riding the buster's trial begins from the moment that the chute opens and the bronc bursts out into the open. The requisite eight seconds he must stay aboard in the bare back class must seem like a lifetime, and some broncs become famous for their ability unfailingly to land their rider in the dirt.

In saddle bronc riding (*left*) the requisite time is ten seconds and in both one hand has to be left free and held high above the horse. Very often (*above*) the bronc manages to rid himself of his rider. Girls compete in rodeo events as well, taking the field in barrel racing (*right*). To turn round the end barrel, having reached it at a flat-out gallop demands agility and a swift response to the rider's commands from the horse, and balance from both of them. Astute horses soon learn the game. Runs are timed and at the collegiate rodeo finals of the United States in 1971 just nine-tenths of a second separated the first ten contestants in the short run.

PONIES

The difference between horses and ponies is often thought to be purely one of size. However not only does the size limit for a pony vary, but there are other equally important differences between them. The normal height limit of a show pony is 14 to 14.2 hands, though the National Pony Society in Britain has accepted animals up to 15.2 hands in height for breeding purposes. Moreover, the beautiful Arabian is classified as a horse the world over, and they are often well below 14 hands, so no hard and fast line can be drawn. It is in temperament, character and general hardiness that ponies differ from horses. They have a compact body, small, sharp pricked ears and usually a rougher coat than a horse, and a definite pony expression which is difficult to describe though instantly recognizable. They can fend for themselves, are sure-footed and clever at getting out of awkward corners. On the whole more intelligent than horses, they often have much more positive characters with more than just a dash of mischievousness, and are capable of giving great affection.

There are of course a vast number of ponies of unidentifiable ancestry and of no particular breed, the result of years of cross breeding, but there are also plenty of specimens of the many different pony breeds that exist throughout the world. On various islands and in specific parts of the world there are still herds of wild ponies roaming over moors all the year round; notable are the celebrated Camargue ponies in southern France, the Shetland ponies that still thrive in the harsh conditions of their native islands, though vast numbers have now been bred in captivity and in warmer conditions to meet popular demand, the Chincoteague ponies of the islands off the Virginian coast, and the Dartmoor and New Forest ponies.

The British Isles are endowed with a wealth of native breeds, and much of the world's high-class pony stock is based upon them. Welsh Mountain ponies are much in demand in America and in South Africa, as they are generally considered to be the most beautiful and stylish of all ponies, having very neat heads much like those of the Arab horses. They also make ideal children's ponies, as do the Dartmoor and the New Forest ponies, all of which have their own particular characteristics. Many famous performers in the show ring and in eventing can trace their ancestry back to these pony stocks, and indeed a good eventing horse needs a drop of pony blood to give him the necessary wits and stamina to cope with the 'natural' fences in a cross country course.

Among other well-known breeds are the Haflinger of Austria, described as a 'Prince in front and a peasant behind', the Appaloosas which are a recognized breed in America, and the Connemara ponies from Ireland.

There are few areas of the world that do not possess at least one native breed of horse or pony but the European continent has such a wide variety of ponies and horses that many other areas of the world have imported breeding stock from Europe in order to improve their standards. Ireland has always been a favourite hunting ground for riding horses and Great Britain has almost unlimited supplies of ponies, hunters and successful competition horses. It is still possible to pick up a bunch of unbroken New Forest ponies at the Beaulieu Road Sales in the New Forest for a reasonable price. But unbroken ponies need expert training and the novice should avoid the temptation of buying an unbroken pony cheaply.

Two of the most famous ponies in the history of the horse world were the South American Criollo ponies Mancha and Gato. These two incredibly tough little animals were the heroes of a fantastic ride of 13,000 miles from Buenos Aires to New York. This ride was undertaken by Aime Tschiffley in the 1920s to prove the stamina of the Criollo pony. The ponies were 15 and 16 years old when the journey began, it lasted two and a half years and the ponies both lived well into their thirties. The Criollo stands about 14 hands high and is usually dun in colour, but skewbalds and piebalds are often found. They have been imported to other parts of the world in large numbers to be trained as polo ponies.

Polo is the oldest of the equestrian games, and is one of the most thrilling forms of organized mounted sport. It is a very exciting game to watch and is even more exciting to play, demanding immense skill and strength always at top speeds, all of which only comes after years of practice. The ponies are very valuable and also need much patient schooling and practice, and polo is thus a very expensive pastime.

Ponies are among the most rewarding of creatures for a family to possess, and give endless pleasure. However, they all need careful looking after and correct feeding and exercising so the responsibility of owning a pony must not be regarded lightly.

The New Forest pony (*right*) has evolved from a mixture of blood. The largest of the British native breeds, anything up to 14.2 hands being acceptable, he is capable of carrying light adults. Their temperament is ideal for children and they are usually quiet in traffic as they see plenty during their life in the Forest.

Most countries of the world have developed their indigenous ponies and in Britain there are a number of breeds in different parts of the land. In addition to the New Forest Pony which still roams free in southern England there are Dartmoor Ponies (*above*), Shetland Ponies (*below*), Welsh Ponies (*left*) and a number more.

The thousands of holidaymakers who travel to the west of England every summer can see the herds of Dartmoor ponies as their road winds over the wild expanse of moor. The Dartmoor pony is small, tough, sure-footed and ideal as a child's first pony. Endowed with a fine head carriage, good presence and an excellent front, he is a good breed to cross with a larger type to produce top-class show ponies and horses. The Dartmoor lives the whole year round on the exposed moorland and is therefore very hardy.

Shetland Ponies, from the group of islands to the far north of Scotland, are probably the oldest and hardiest of Britain's native breeds and rarely grow much above three feet even when living on good grass in the south as opposed to the sparse grazing and hard climate of their native islands. Their popularity grows continually and there are now three types of Shetland bred in America; for riding, for draught events and for driving.

Welsh Mountain Ponies are very agile and sure-footed as they were bred to live in rough steep areas. This, along with their gentle nature, makes them very popular as children's ponies. They are also very attractive in appearance, due to infusions of Arab blood in past years. This gives the Welsh Mountain Pony a slightly dish-faced look, like the Arab. There are other types of Welsh ponies, such as the Welsh Cob, which is a larger animal, and the Welsh Pony, which was originally created by crossing the Cob with the Mountain Pony.

Highland Ponies (*left*) are handsome stocky animals and were much esteemed by Queen Victoria for their endurance and reliability in carrying stags across the deer forests of Scotland. They make excellent pack ponies and also go well in harness classes. This attractive creamy colouring with black mane and tails is called dun, and often the ponies have a black dorsal stripe and black stockings.

One of the native ponies of Europe is the sure-footed Haflinger of Austria (*top right*). This mountain breed, easily recognized by their rich chestnut colour and long, flowing, cream-coloured manes and tails, is strong and hard-working which has made it popular in many other countries. Their evolution is uncertain but modern Haflingers are known to carry the blood of a half-bred Arab. They are renowned for their longevity, often working for 40 years, and can be seen in the Tyrol pulling loads of hay in summer, when the grass is dried on rails or around a pole, or hauling logs from the pine forests. In winter they make attractive sleigh horses wearing studded shoes and bearing jingling bells upon their harness.

Polo ponies (*below right*) are all called ponies even though the abolition of a height limit for the game now means that many taking part are really horses of as much as 16 hands. They need to be quick, agile, obedient and courageous and smaller ponies generally prove to be the best. Both pony and rider must be highly skilled to play this fast-moving and dangerous game which originated in Persia and was introduced to Britain by soldiers who learned it in India in the middle of the last century. Prince Philip, the Duke of Edinburgh, was a regular player until a wrist injury forced him to give up the game. Prince Charles has followed in his father's footsteps and enjoys a game whenever he can find time to play.

Riding ponies are often half-bred and the introduction of Arab blood will often be evident in an elegance lacking in most indigenous ponies (*left*). Good grooming and well fitted and carefully kept harness help to present a smart, well turned out appearance.

Some people believe that the beautiful wild ponies of the Camargue (*this page and overleaf*) carry some oriental blood, which is quite possible since Arab horses introduced to Spain may well have found their way to this wild part of southern France. These semi-wild white ponies, probably descended from prehistoric horses, roam free among the lagoons and coastal marshes of the Rhône delta. Local farmers periodically round them up to brand them and check condition and numbers, and some are broken in to farm work and to act as cow ponies to herd the black Camargue bulls.

For a foal (*left*) giving one's back a good scratch presents no problems but when this New Forest Pony grows older he will not find it quite so easy. Fences, gates, branches and often humans are considered ideal scratching posts by horses, and they will practically knock you over as they rub up and down in the small of your back.

The true Romany gypsies were the traditional horse dealers of the world but they are now a vanishing race and the few that are left are more likely to have a smart modern trailer caravan behind a motor vehicle than the traditional horse-drawn, gaily painted caravan. But some do still survive (*right and below*) and young Romanies grow up with a sense of horsemanship even if they may have some difficulty in getting this Gypsy pony between the shafts.

Ponies are sociable creatures and love to hang over a gate watching any goings on (*left*), like this Palomino half asleep in the sun. If their grazing is isolated it is best for them to have company of some kind, either another pony or horse, and they can be turned out with a dairy herd or a flock of sheep.

Young riders must be taught the proper care of their mounts, and to show their appreciation for a pony's hard work. Feeding ponies before turning them loose to graze in a field (*right*) is a fitting end to a day's riding.

Riders need just as much training as ponies—probably rather more. Here a pupil is being taught balance and a good, firm seat by trotting without help of stirrup irons or reins (*below*). To increase the rider's confidence the pony is being held on a lunge rein.

LOOKING AFTER HORSES

If the modern horse, like his wild ancestors, could have unlimited acreages of grazing including grasses, herbs and shrubs in such variety as to constitute a balanced diet, and constant fresh water, and did not have to work at speed or over obstacles under the weight of a rider, he would exist satisfactorily enough. In the spring and summer, when the grass is at its peak nutrient value and the weather is warm, he would grow fat and sleek; in the cold winds and wet of winter, when food is scarce, he would lose condition and strength, as did his forebears. But today's horse, his liberty restricted and expected to gallop and jump, requires supplementary energy-producing foods to that obtained from grassland.

Ponies are usually endowed with stamina and incredible hardiness and need far less mollycoddling than their larger brothers whose veins may hold a fairly high percentage of Thoroughbred and Arab blood. Indeed, the pony thrives better if kept out all the year round and is perfectly happy in weather that would reduce many larger horses to shivering misery. But, despite his toughness, a pony cannot live on air nor in a tiny bare paddock.

If he is kept on his own (which is not really a good idea since most of all he needs company of his own kind) the paddock needs to be of about three acres of well drained ground. If less, more extra food will have to be given, and there is a danger of a small piece of ground becoming a mud patch in winter. Ponies are rarely unsound but they can get mud-fever (a painful skin irritation on the legs and belly), cracked heels (when the skin becomes chapped) or thrush (an unpleasant, rotting condition of the feet caused by dirty standings) just as easily as any other equine. The grass must be of fairly good quality, of the sort found in old pasture land, and the ground and hedges free from those poisonous plants which are so fatally attractive to horses and ponies. The most common poisonous plants are *ragwort*, with its yellow flower, most of the *buttercup* family, which horses will eat if the rest of the grazing is poor; *foxglove*, *monkshood*, *black briony* and, of course, the most deadly of all, the English *yew*.

Natural hedges make good fences. They afford shelter and act as a windbreak. Next best are wooden posts and rails, but a cheaper fence, and almost as good, can be made from heavy gauge wire stretched tightly between strong posts with the lower strand not less than one foot from the ground.

An open field shelter, sited to face away from prevailing winds, is advisable. The pony may not use it in winter, preferring to stand either in its lee or under a natural protection, but in summer he will go into it more in order to keep away from flies. The paddock must be kept clear of cans, bits of wire, glass, etc. which might cause injury, and there must be an adequate supply of clean water. This is best provided by a field pipe to a trough which has no sharp edges and can be emptied for cleaning. Water is as essential as solid food (it is eighty per cent of the horse's body). A horse or pony can do without food for as much as thirty days but deprived entirely of water he will die in about a quarter of that time.

In summer the pony will be content with only grass if not doing much work—but such is the perversity of ponies and horses that too much grass is almost as bad as too little. Apart from being too fat to exert himself at anything more than a plodding walk, an overweight horse or pony can develop a painful disease of the feet, laminitis, which is an acute inflammation inside the outer casing of the hoof affecting the sensitive laminae. If a pony gets too fat deny him access to the luscious grass. Use the field shelter to confine him during the day and put him out at night. If he still adds weight restrict his grazing to a few hours each day. Do not gallop him until he has lost his surplus weight and is in harder condition. Fat ponies must be conditioned gradually and exercised at a walk and slow trot, or the effort may be too much for their wind and legs.

Food is needed for four things: to maintain body temperature ($100°$–$101.5°$F in the horse); replace natural tissue wastage; build up and maintain body condition; and supply energy needed for movement and internal processes such as digestion.

If food is short and the weather cold the first two requirements will take the lion's share and the last two will get next to nothing. As a result the animal gets thin and loses strength and energy. Even when food is plentiful and all four requirements are satisfied, the animal's condition will suffer if he is made to work hard and expend a lot of energy. The working pony or horse must, therefore, have an input of energy food to match his expenditure of energy.

Energy is produced by foods like beans and peas, oats and to a slightly lesser extent barley. Maize, also, is heat and energy giving. Such foods are not natural to a digestive system designed to cope with herbage. To be digested they need bulk and roughage. For the hard-worked pony grass adequately provides this bulk.

A sudden change to a richer diet can be dangerous for horses and ponies, especially the pure native mountain (*right*) and moorland breeds which were developed on the sparsest grazing and cannot cope with a large supply of lush, sweet summer grass without running the risk of laminitis and other problems.

Energy is probably best supplied by oats but unfortunately oats do not really suit ponies, since they frequently become quite unmanageable on even a handful a day, while the smell of beans and peas is enough to make them spend half their time bucking, kicking and standing on their hind legs. The answer to the problem is to restrict the grazing to a reasonable level and feed one or another of the proprietary brands of pony nuts and cubes which, in some instances, are a complete balanced diet in themselves. A ration of 3lb of nuts per day mixed with 1lb of bran, which contains a high percentage of essential salts, and a double handful of chaff (a mixture of chopped oat straw and hay) and fed damped should keep a pony of 13 hands sufficiently energetic.

In the autumn the grass loses its goodness and new growth does not appear until the spring. Hay should be fed throughout the winter months. The feed that kept him energetic in summer will now suffice in winter when he is not doing so much work. Sliced carrots, not chopped ones which might lodge in the gullet, apples etc. can be added to the concentrate feed to add variety, but *not* household scraps. Incidentally, if grass is short resist any temptation to offer the contents of the lawn-mower box. The pony will probably be delighted but the result may be disastrous and cause severe colic. It is wise to give ponies their ration in a haynet (a small one in the morning and a larger at evening) and to string it as high as possible, well out of the way of a pawing fore-foot. A block of salt should always be kept in the field to provide vitamins deficient in pasture or food. If a pony being fed and on reasonable grazing looks generally listless and not well it is likely that he has worms, in particular red worms. These parasites are always present in domestic horses and on their pastures, the latter being the principle vehicle in their life cycle. By managing the grass correctly, resting fields regularly and grazing horses with cattle in a rotational system, the worms can be controlled. Horses are bad grazers, being very selective, but cattle are the ideal vacuum-cleaner and they do not act as host to the red worms they ingest. But pasture management is impracticable for the majority of one- or two-horse owners, who can often do no more than remove droppings regularly. It is important that this be done since it is in them that the worm eggs pass out of the body; they then develop and regain entry into the system from the pasture, and so the cycle begins again.

The main attack against the red worm must be by dosing. A veterinary surgeon will advise on dosage and frequency after taking an egg count from a sample of dung. Heavy infestation can result in anaemia, pro-

Horses are so built that they should eat little and often and thus they can happily spend most of the day grazing. This chestnut (*left*) obviously thinks his bay companion is monopolizing a much tastier patch of grass!

nounced loss of condition and even death.

A pony's winter coat provides a waterproof protection against the worst weather when it is fully grown, as does the formation of a layer of grease next to the skin. It is therefore wrong to clean and groom the pony thoroughly during the winter. A quick brush over with a dandy brush to remove the worst of the mud will not interfere with the natural layer of grease.

Each day and every day, whatever the weather, a pony must be inspected to see that all is well and that water is available. In summer twigs, leaves and scum may have to be removed from the drinking trough and in winter there may be ice to clear from the surface.

The last item in the pony's welfare is the care of his feet. It is possible to ride ponies without shoes if they never come off soft going but in general a working pony needs to be shod if he is not to become foot-sore on hard roads and stony tracks. Once a month his shoes will need to be removed, whether they are worn out or not, the feet trimmed and cut back, and the shoes replaced either with the old set or with a new one. Neglected feet are more prone to becoming diseased and may, indeed, cause quite severe injury if they are allowed to become too long or if the nail clenches rise up and protrude beyond the wall of the hoof. In both the last instances the pony can cut itself with its own feet.

Ponies of the mountain and moorland breeds or those containing a large proportion of native blood will live out all the year very well but those of more aristocratic lineage, the Thoroughbred and the various Arab crosses, are not always so well suited to the rigours of cold and wet weather and do not grow such a thick protective coat. Usually they will need stabling, at least at night, a proceeding involving much extra work, but if they have to live out it may be necessary to provide them with a waterproof New Zealand type rug—and that, too, involves a lot more work and attention. They will also need larger rations of concentrate foods than the more self-sufficient natives.

Horses, as distinct from ponies, may be expected to be in harder work and for them stabling is frequently a necessity. In days gone by, when hunting was the *raison d'être* for keeping a horse, hunters were put out to grass in May and not brought into the stable until September. The increase in competitive riding has now changed that routine and the majority of horses work throughout the year, being given only a matter of a few weeks when they are entirely at grass. In some ways this arrangement is beneficial since the horse has little or no opportunity to lose his hard condition, whereas the horse out for the whole summer becomes so fat and flabby that an extended period of quiet exercise is necessary to get him into a suitable condition to work at fast paces.

In the case of horses laid off work for the whole summer management need go no further than the provision of a shelter and regular inspection, with particular attention being paid to the condition of the feet. Usually shoes are removed altogether but it is probably better sense to shoe with 'grass tips', an attenuated form of the shoe proper, to prevent the foot breaking. No additional feeding is necessary beyond that obtained from the grass.

The management of a working horse during the summer will vary according to what is expected of him. A horse used purely for light hacking might be stabled during the day and put out at night and would require little or no extra feeding apart from a small concentrate feed and a little hay to keep him occupied during the period spent in his box. For the horse competing regularly, however, a more sophisticated and time-consuming routine has to be devised which will be nearer to the programme carried out in the winter months. Clearly such programmes depend very much on individual circumstances.

The object of stabling horses, or keeping them under what is called the combined method, where the horse goes out for part of the day in a New Zealand rug to do his own exercising, is so that they may be more easily and effectively conditioned for a particular purpose, such as hunting.

In every case a loose box is preferable to the old-fashioned stall, which involves the horse being tied up in a comparatively narrow space, facing a blank wall. Nothing could be better calculated to produce a neurotic horse. The bigger the box the better, and it must be airy.

Doors, divided into top and bottom sections, the former being fastened back to the outside of the building or even dispensed with altogether, must open outwards otherwise it can be impossible to get into the box if either straw becomes jammed against the inside or, even worse, if the horse should be lying across the entrance.

The height of the bottom door needs to be sufficient to discourage any thought of jumping out but low

Horses ridden on roads and other hard going need shoeing to prevent the foot becoming sore or breaking away. Farriers are highly skilled and frequently fit the shoes while the metal is still hot (*left*) to ensure an exact fit.

Horses love companionship (*right*) and on the whole make friends easily, though they can take strong dislikes and have to be separated. A broken horse that has to live alone is always very dependent on his owner and will be lonely without any company at all.

enough to allow the horse to stand with his head out without having to crane his neck. A height of 4–4½ ft is about right with a width of at least 4 ft.

Ideally boxes should face south and be sited so that the inmates can see as much as possible of what is going on around them.

Ventilation will be amply catered for if the top door is always left open but draughts, as much an anathema to the horse as the human, must be rigidly excluded. They cause aches and pains and contribute materially to colds and chills. Extra ventilation can be obtained from a window of the type that swings inwards from the base so that air enters in an upward stream and not directly on the horse, or by louvres, set high in the rear wall, to take away the rising bad air which can accumulate. Windows, of course, as well as light switches must be protected by a grill of some sort. Fresh air never hurt a horse and it is better in cold weather to give an extra rug and more feed than to shut the top door.

Use materials which keep the building relatively cool in summer and correspondingly warm in winter. Wooden structures for this reason are best lined inside. Avoid corrugated iron sheeting as a roof. It attracts heat and doesn't keep out cold. The drainage problem is best overcome by making a slightly sloping concrete floor and an open drain *outside* the stable door.

Equipment in the box should be confined to essentials; a ring set in the wall for tying up and receptacles for food and water. For bedding use wheat straw and also peat moss and sawdust for those animals who eat their beds to the detriment of their wind. Use sufficient of whatever type to encourage a horse to lie down. Soiled areas must be cleaned out each day and droppings picked up as a matter of course whenever you go into the box.

A long winter coat would make a stabled horse sweat excessively, and lose flesh if he is worked hard, so he must have his coat removed by clipping and the loss

Feet must be carefully looked after (*left*). They should be cleaned out with a hoof pick and the outside brushed with hoof oil to prevent them cracking. Every four weeks or so the shoes should be removed, whether worn or not, and the foot rasped to its proper shape.

Mud and dirt is best got out of a thick coat with a dandy brush, although this coarse brush is sometimes too ticklish for a thin-skinned thoroughbred or clipped-out coat. This should be followed by the body-brush used in strong circular strokes all over the body and for the forelock, mane and tail (*top*).

Keeping tack in good condition is important too (*above*). As well as lengthening the life of the leather it keeps it soft and supple so that the horse does not develop body sores from its chafing.

93

made good by rugs. He will then need a balanced diet to build up his body and supply muscle as well as energy for his work. Exercise and grooming are also essential. The first develops and strengthens the working muscles, hardens the sinews and tendons of the legs and keeps his wind in good order. The second not only helps in the development and toning of the muscles but it cleans the body so that it can work with full efficiency.

A stabled horse, it must be recognized, is kept under artificial conditions and because of the energy demands of his work he consumes large quantities of artificial food. His body, as a result, is required to deal with a greater quantity of waste matter. Much of it will be disposed of through excrement and the increased rate of breathing by the lungs, but almost as much is dispersed through the skin. It is necessary, therefore, to keep the skin clean if it is to perform this necessary function.

The horse's stomach is designed to take food slowly and almost continuously over long periods. It is vital therefore that a horse be fed *little and often*, remembering that his stomach cannot cope with concentrate feeds of more than 4lb at one sitting. A horse should *never* be worked immediately after a meal.

About an hour must be given for the digestive process to be completed for the stomach is placed behind the diaphragm, which is in contact with the lungs in front and with the stomach and liver at the rear. Immediately after a feed the stomach becomes distended and pressure, through the diaphragm, will be exerted on the lungs. This will cause no trouble to the horse at rest but should he be worked fast in this condition his breathing will be impaired and interference will be caused to the digestive process. At best the horse may develop colic of varying severity, at worst the lungs could choke with blood and a rupture of the stomach occur.

For the stabled horse a balanced diet will comprise foods of three groups—*bulk*, *energy* and what may be termed *auxiliaries*. In combination these must produce five constituents: *proteins*; *fats*, *starches* and *sugar*; *fibrous roughage*; *salts*, *vitamins*, and, of course, *water* is equally essential.

Bulk is provided principally by hay, which is high in its fibrous content-matter as well as containing relatively high percentages of protein, salts, etc. Energy foods containing starches and fats, etc., as well as other constituents are for practical purposes, oats, maize, barley, etc., of which the former is preferred. Nuts and cubes, of course, can also be classified under this heading. Auxiliaries are such items as bran, containing a high percentage of salts, linseed (a fattening food) and the various forms of *green* food—carrots and other suitable roots. In addition in this group we can include the various feed-additives, designed to repair mineral and vitamin deficiencies, cod liver oil (a conditioner), molasses, glucose and even seaweed concentrates.

The problem, of course, is in feeding the three groups in the right proportions and in this respect horses are decidedly individual making it impossible to lay down hard and fast rules. As a guide we can take it that a horse of about 16.2 hands will need a daily intake of food of about 28lb. For a horse in regular work and perhaps hunting one day per week the proportion of bulk to the remaining two constituents of the diet would be about half and half. A horse in lighter work could be given a greater quantity of bulk food and less energy foods whilst, conversely, a horse in fast work, such as racing, would require more energy food and less bulk, although the latter will never fall below one-third of the total intake, since a large amount of energy food cannot be accommodated without its presence.

In all cases energy foods must be discontinued if work is forced to cease for any reason. A hunter, however, would normally be expected to be in receipt of around 10lb of oats per day, or the equivalent in nuts and cubes, which would be given in a number of feeds and mixed with bran, etc. The hay ration which is eaten and digested slowly is usually given in two lots, the bulk as a late feed to keep the horse happy through the night hours.

The rule about watering used to be *water before feeding* but modern practice holds that it is better to keep a constant supply of water with the horse and this is the system most usually followed.

The stabled horse, therefore, demands as much attention as a human baby and probably more! He will need feeding five times a day, at least one hour's grooming and two hours' exercise and in addition at least a further hour will be spent in making up his bed and cleaning out the stable. A certain amount of labour can be avoided by turning out the horse during the day in a waterproof, New Zealand type rug, and this is a convenient method for those whose time is limited and will reduce the period spent at exercise as well as making cleaning out an easier job. Then, of course, he has to be clipped, usually twice during autumn and winter, and his mane and tail must be pulled and made tidy. And he will need worming at the beginning of the season and shoeing regularly.

All in all it's a far cry from the little paddock and living on grass. Who said that the horse was the servant of man?

Horses need regular exercise. Racehorses are taken out whatever the weather (*right*). Often it is only walking, which is one of the best paces for getting a horse fit, combined with the occasional trot and short sharp burst at a faster speed, known as a 'pipe-opener'. Warmly rugged-up they will leave their stable yard in the early morning for their prescribed amount of exercise.

INDEX

Figures in italics refer to the illustrations

Acknowledgments

The publishers would like to thank the following individuals and organizations for their kind permission to reproduce the pictures in this book:

American Saddle Horse Breeders Association: 24 above; Animal Photography: 17 above, 19 above, 20 above, 21, 40 centre, 77 above, 87, 92; Ardea Photographics: 4–5; Associated Freelance Artists: 17 below, 30 below, 79 above; Australian News & Information Bureau: 65 below; Barnaby's Picture Library: 31, 75 above; Bavaria Verlag: 66 below; Judith Campbell: 85 above; John Carnemolla: 15, jacket front centre right; Bruce Coleman: 24 below; Colour Library International: 25, 39 below, 63, 64 left, jacket back; Arthur Dailey: 65 above; C. M. Dixon: 8; Fox Photos: 39 above; Susan Griggs (Adam Woolfitt): 68 above, 70 above and below; Michael Holford: 9 above and below, 10–11, 23; Dan Hubber: 69 right; Elizabeth Johnson: 13 above; Keystone Press Agency: 22 above, 32 above, 33, 35, 38 below, 46 left, 64 right, 79 below; E. D.

Lacey: 22 below, 36, 37, 38 above, 40 above, 41 above and centre, 42 below, 45, 46 right, 47 right, 48 above and centre, 49, 50 above, jacket front above right; Colin Lofting: 69 above and left; James Fain Logan: 71; London Express News & Feature Service: 95; Jane Miller: 1, 26, jacket front left; John Moss: 77 below, 85 below, 93 below, jacket front below right; Octopus Books: 12 below; Daniel O'Keefe: 7, 68 below; Walter D Osborne: 14 above and below, 40 below, 41 below; Van Phillips: 53, 5: above and below; Popperfoto: 88; Rapho: 80–81; Peter Roberts: 54, 67 75 below, 76; W. W. Rouch & Co.: 42 above; Ianthe Ruthven: 13 below; Spanish Riding School of Vienna: 56, 57 above and below, 58, 59; Spectrum Colour Library: 2–3, 12 above, 28, 29, 30 above, 32 below, 43 below, 60, 61, 66 above, 73, 82, 83 above and below, 84, 90, 91, 93 above, endpapers; Tony Stone Associates: 74; Syndication International: 48 below, 50 below, 51; U.S. Trotting Association: 43 above; Elisabeth Weiland: 18; Barbara Woodhouse: 78.